Blessings and Prayers for Confirmation

A Devotional Companion

CONCORDIA PUBLISHING HOUSE · SAINT LOUIS

Congratulations! The fact that you are reading the introduction to this small book indicates that in all likelihood you recently confirmed your faith in Christ through the Rite of Confirmation. For those who were brought to the Christian faith through the Sacrament of Holy Baptism as infants, you doubtless have no memory of the event. At that time, your parents and/or sponsors spoke a number of promises on your behalf. Now you have made these same promises and declarations in your confirmation. To help you remember these promises, this book begins with the orders for Baptism and Confirmation.

Blessings and Prayers

for Confirmation is designed to help you remember the promises you spoke and to prepare you for the daily challenges that face many young people. As you read and meditate upon the words of the psalms, the brief devotions, the prayers, and the other resources contained between the covers of *Blessings and Prayers for Confirmation*, we pray that you may be strengthened by God's Holy Spirit as we walk together in faith.

Contents

Order of Holy Baptism

Stand

P In the name of the Father and of the ✠ Son and of the Holy Spirit. Matthew 28:19b

C **Amen.**

P Dearly beloved, Christ our Lord says in the last chapter of Matthew, "All authority in heaven and on earth has been given to Me. Therefore go and make disciples of all nations, baptizing them in the name of the Father and of the Son and of the Holy Spirit." In the last chapter of Mark our Lord promises, "Whoever believes and is baptized will be saved." And the apostle Peter has written, "Baptism now saves you." Matthew 28:18b–19; Mark 16:16a; 1 Peter 3:21

The Word of God also teaches that we are all conceived and born sinful and are under the power of the devil until Christ claims us as His own. We would be lost forever unless delivered from sin, death, and everlasting condemnation. But the Father of all mercy and grace has sent His Son Jesus Christ, who atoned for the sin of the whole world, that whoever believes in Him should not perish but have eternal life.

The pastor addresses each candidate:

P How are you named?

R *Name*

The pastor makes the sign of the holy cross upon the forehead and heart of each candidate while saying:

P *Name*, receive the sign of the holy cross both upon your ✠ forehead and upon your ✠ heart to mark you as one redeemed by Christ the crucified.

P Let us pray.

Almighty and eternal God, according to Your strict judgment You condemned the unbelieving world through the flood, yet according to Your great mercy You preserved believing Noah and his family, eight souls in all. You drowned hard-hearted Pharaoh and all his host in the Red Sea, yet led Your people Israel through the water on dry ground, foreshadowing this washing of Your Holy Baptism. Through the Baptism in the Jordan of Your beloved Son, our Lord Jesus Christ, You sanctified and instituted all waters to be a blessed flood and a lavish washing away of sin. We pray that You would behold *name(s)* according to Your boundless mercy and bless *him/her/them* with true faith by the Holy Spirit, that through this saving flood all sin in *him/her/them*, which has been inherited from Adam and which *he himself/she herself/they themselves has/have* committed since, would be drowned and die. Grant that *he/she/they* be kept safe and secure in the holy ark of the Christian Church, being separated from the multitude of unbelievers and serving Your name at all times with a fervent spirit and a joyful hope, so that,

with all believers in Your promise, _he/she/_
they would be declared worthy of eternal
life; through Jesus Christ, our Lord.

C **Amen.**

_If the sponsors were previously enrolled, the service continues
below with the Holy Gospel._

P From ancient times the Church has
observed the custom of appointing sponsors
for baptismal candidates and catechumens.
In the Evangelical Lutheran Church sponsors
are to confess the faith expressed in the
Apostles' Creed and taught in the Small
Catechism. They are, whenever possible, to
witness the Baptism of those they sponsor.
They are to pray for them, support them in
their ongoing instruction and nurture in the
Christian faith, and encourage them toward
the faithful reception of the Lord's Supper.
They are at all times to be examples to them
of the holy life of faith in Christ and love for
the neighbor.

The pastor addresses the sponsors.

P Is it your intention to serve *name of candidate(s)* as sponsors in the Christian faith?

R *Yes, with the help of God.*

P God enable you both to will and to do this faithful and loving work and with His grace fulfill what we are unable to do.

C **Amen.**

P Hear the Holy Gospel according to St. Mark.

They brought young children to [Jesus] that He might touch them; but the disciples rebuked those who brought them. But when Jesus saw it, He was greatly displeased and said to them, "Let the little children come to Me, and do not forbid them; for of such is the kingdom of God. Assuredly, I say to you, whoever does not receive the kingdom of God as a little child will by no means enter it." And He took them up in His arms, put His hands on them, and blessed them.

Mark 10:13–16 NKJV

P This is the Word of the Lord.

C Thanks be to God.

The pastor places his hands on the head(s) of the candidate(s), and the congregation joins in praying:

C Our Father who art in heaven,
hallowed be Thy name,
Thy kingdom come,
Thy will be done on earth as it is in
heaven;
give us this day our daily bread;
and forgive us our trespasses as we
forgive those who trespass against us;
and lead us not into temptation,
but deliver us from evil.   Matthew 6:9–13

For Thine is the kingdom and the power
and the glory forever and ever. Amen.

If the baptismal party has stood at the entrance of the nave to this point, they now move to the font. A hymn may be sung during the procession. Then the pastor says:

P The Lord preserve your coming in and your
going out from this time forth and even ✠
forevermore.

C **Amen.**

Sit

The pastor addresses the candidate(s) and asks the following questions:

P <u>*Name(s)*</u>, do you renounce the devil?

R *Yes, I renounce him.*

P Do you renounce all his works?

R *Yes, I renounce them.*

P Do you renounce all his ways?

R *Yes, I renounce them.*

P Do you believe in God, the Father Almighty, maker of heaven and earth?

R *Yes, I believe.*

P Do you believe in Jesus Christ, His only Son, our Lord, who was conceived by the Holy Spirit, born of the virgin Mary, suffered under Pontius Pilate, was crucified, died and was buried; He descended into hell; the third day He rose again from the dead; He ascended into heaven and sits at the right hand of God the Father Almighty; from thence He will come to judge the living and the dead?

R *Yes, I believe.*

P Do you believe in the Holy Spirit, the holy Christian Church, the communion of saints, the forgiveness of sins, the resurrection of the body, and the life everlasting?

R *Yes, I believe.*

P *Name*, do you desire to be baptized?

R *Yes, I do.*

The pastor pours water three times on the head of each candidate while saying:

P *Name*, I baptize you in the name of the Father and of the Son and of the Holy Spirit.

C **Amen.**

The pastor places his hands on the head of the newly baptized while saying:

P The almighty God and Father of our Lord Jesus Christ, who has given you the new birth of water and of the Spirit and has forgiven you all your sins, strengthen you with His grace to life ✠ everlasting.

C **Amen.**

P Receive this white garment to show that you have been clothed with the robe of Christ's righteousness that covers all your sin. So shall you stand without fear before the judgment seat of Christ to receive the inheritance prepared for you from the foundation of the world.

P Receive this burning light to show that you have received Christ who is the Light of the world. Live always in the light of Christ, and be ever watchful for His coming, that you may meet Him with joy and enter with Him into the marriage feast of the Lamb in His kingdom, which shall have no end.

A In Holy Baptism God the Father has made you *a member/members* of His Son, our Lord Jesus Christ, and *an heir/heirs* with us of all the treasures of heaven in the one holy Christian and apostolic Church. We receive you in Jesus' name as our *brother(s)/sister(s)* in Christ, that together we might hear His Word, receive His gifts, and proclaim the praises of Him who called us out of darkness into His marvelous light.

C **Amen. We welcome you in the name of the Lord.**

Stand

P Let us pray.

Almighty and most merciful God and Father, we thank and praise You that You graciously preserve and enlarge Your family and have granted *name(s)* the new birth in Holy Baptism and made *him/her/them a member/members* of Your Son, our Lord Jesus Christ, and *an heir/heirs* of Your

17

heavenly kingdom. We humbly implore You that, as *he/she/they has/have* now become Your *child/children*, You would keep *him/her/them* in *his/her/their* baptismal grace, that according to Your good pleasure *he/she/they* may faithfully grow to lead a godly life to the praise and honor of Your holy name and finally, with all Your saints, obtain the promised inheritance in heaven; through Jesus Christ, our Lord.

C **Amen.**

P Peace ✠ be with you.

C **Amen.**

All return to their places.

Rite of
Confirmation

P Beloved in the Lord, our Lord Jesus Christ said to His apostles: "All authority has been given to Me in heaven and on earth. Therefore go and make disciples of all nations, baptizing them in the name of the Father and of the Son and of the Holy Spirit, teaching them to observe all things that I have commanded you; and lo, I am with you always, even to the end of the age." You have been baptized and catechized in the Christian faith according to our Lord's bidding. Jesus said, "Whoever confesses Me before men, I will also confess before My Father who is in heaven. But whoever denies Me before men, I will also deny before My Father who is in heaven." Lift up your hearts, therefore, to the God of all grace and joyfully give answer to what I now ask you in the name of the Lord. *Matthew 28:18b–20 NKJV; Matthew 10:32–33 NKJV alt.*

P Do you this day in the presence of God

and of this congregation acknowledge the gifts that God gave you in your Baptism?

R Yes, I do.

P Do you renounce the devil?

R Yes, I renounce him.

P Do you renounce all his works?

R Yes, I renounce them.

P Do you renounce all his ways?

R Yes, I renounce them.

P Do you believe in God, the Father Almighty?

R Yes, I believe in God, the Father Almighty, maker of heaven and earth.

P Do you believe in Jesus Christ, His only Son, our Lord?

R Yes, I believe in Jesus Christ, His only Son, our Lord, who was conceived by the Holy Spirit, born of the virgin Mary, suffered under Pontius Pilate, was crucified, died, and was buried. He descended into hell. The third day He rose again from the dead. He ascended into heaven and sits at the right hand of God the Father Almighty. From thence He will come to judge the living and the dead.

P Do you believe in the Holy Spirit?

R Yes, I believe in the Holy Spirit, the holy Christian Church, the communion of saints, the forgiveness of sins, the resurrection of the body, and the life everlasting.

P Do you hold all the prophetic and apostolic Scriptures to be the inspired Word of God?

R I do.

P Do you confess the doctrine of the Evangelical Lutheran Church, drawn from the Scriptures, as you have learned to know it from the Small Catechism, to be faithful and true?

R I do.

P Do you intend to hear the Word of God

and receive the Lord's Supper faithfully?

R I do, by the grace of God.

P Do you intend to live according to the Word of God, and in faith, word, and deed to remain true to God, Father, Son, and Holy Spirit, even to death?

R I do, by the grace of God.

P Do you intend to continue steadfast in this confession and Church and to suffer all, even death, rather than fall away from it?

R I do, by the grace of God.

P We rejoice with thankful hearts that you have been baptized and have received the teaching of the Lord. You have confessed the faith and been absolved of your sins. As you continue to hear the Lord's Word and receive His blessed Sacrament, He who has begun a good work in you will bring it to completion at the day of Jesus Christ.

C **Amen.**

The catechumens kneel to receive the confirmation blessing.
The pastor places his hands on the head of each catechumen
and makes the sign of the cross on the forehead while saying:

P **_Name_**, the almighty God and Father of our Lord Jesus Christ, who has given you the new birth of water and of the Spirit and has forgiven you all your sins, strengthen you with His grace to life ✠ everlasting.

R *Amen.*

The pastor may read a text of Holy Scripture
as a remembrance of confirmation.
After all the catechumens have received the blessing,
one or both of the following collects are prayed.

Stand

P Let us pray.

Lord God, heavenly Father, we thank and praise You for Your great goodness in bringing these Your sons and daughters to the knowledge of Your Son, our Savior, Jesus Christ, and enabling them both with the heart to believe and with the mouth to confess His saving name. Grant that, bringing forth the fruits of faith, they may continue steadfast and victorious to the day when all who have fought the good fight of faith shall receive the crown of righteousness; through Jesus Christ, Your Son, our Lord, who lives and reigns with You and the Holy Spirit, one God, now and forever.

C **Amen.**

P Almighty and most merciful Father, in the waters of Holy Baptism You have united Your children in the suffering and death of Your Son, Jesus Christ, cleansing them by His blood. Renew in them the gift of Your Holy Spirit, that they may live in daily contrition and repentance with a faith that ever clings to their Savior. Deliver them from the power of Satan and preserve them from false and dangerous doctrines, that they may remain faithful in hearing Christ's Word and receiving His body and blood. By the Lord's Supper strengthen them to believe that no one can make satisfaction for sin but Christ alone. Enable them to find joy and comfort only in Him, learning from this Sacrament to love You and their neighbor and to bear their cross with patience and joy until the day of the resurrection of their bodies to life immortal; through Jesus Christ, Your Son, our Lord, who lives and reigns with You and the Holy Spirit, one God, now and forever.

C **Amen.**

P Peace ✠ be with you.

C **Amen.**

A Collection of
Favorite Psalms

Blessed is the man
who walks not in the counsel of
the wicked,
nor stands in the way of sinners,
nor sits in the seat of scoffers;
²but his delight is in the law of
the LORD,
and on His law he meditates
day and night.
³He is like a tree
planted by streams of water
that yields its fruit in its season,
and its leaf does not wither.
In all that he does, he prospers.
⁴The wicked are not so,
but are like chaff that the wind
drives away.
⁵Therefore the wicked will not
stand in the judgment,
nor sinners in the congregation
of the righteous;
⁶for the LORD knows the way of
the righteous,
but the way of the wicked will
perish.

O Lord, our Lord,
how majestic is Your name in
all the earth!
You have set Your glory above the
heavens.
²Out of the mouth of babes and
infants,
You have established strength
because of Your foes,
to still the enemy and the
avenger.
³When I look at Your heavens, the
work of Your fingers,
the moon and the stars, which
You have set in place,
⁴what is man that You are mindful
of him,
and the son of man that You
care for him?
⁵Yet You have made him a little
lower than the heavenly
beings
and crowned him with glory
and honor.
⁶You have given him dominion

over the works of Your
hands;
You have put all things under
his feet,
⁷all sheep and oxen,
and also the beasts of the field,
⁸the birds of the heavens, and the
fish of the sea,
whatever passes along the paths
of the seas.
⁹O Lᴏʀᴅ, our Lord,
how majestic is Your name in all the earth!

The fool says in his heart,
"There is no God."
They are corrupt, they do
abominable deeds,
there is none who does good.
²The Lord looks down from
heaven on the children of
man,
to see if there are any who
understand,
who seek after God.
³They have all turned aside;
together they have become
corrupt;
there is none who does good,
not even one.
⁴Have they no knowledge, all the
evildoers
who eat up my people as they
eat bread
and do not call upon the Lord?
⁵There they are in great terror,
for God is with the generation
of the righteous.
⁶You would shame the plans

of the poor,
but the L ORD is his refuge.
⁷Oh, that salvation for Israel would
come out of Zion!
When the L ORD restores the
fortunes of His people,
let Jacob rejoice, let Israel be
glad.

The Lord is my shepherd; I
shall not want.
²He makes me lie down in green
pastures.
He leads me beside still waters.
³He restores my soul.
He leads me in paths of
righteousness
for His name's sake.
⁴Even though I walk through the
valley of the shadow of
death,
I will fear no evil,
for You are with me;
Your rod and Your staff,
they comfort me.
⁵You prepare a table before me
in the presence of my enemies;
You anoint my head with oil;
my cup overflows.
⁶Surely goodness and mercy shall
follow me
all the days of my life,
and I shall dwell in the house of the Lord
forever.

The LORD is my light and my
salvation;
whom shall I fear?
The LORD is the stronghold of my
life;
of whom shall I be afraid?
²When evildoers assail me
to eat up my flesh,
my adversaries and foes,
it is they who stumble and fall.
³Though an army encamp
against me,
my heart shall not fear;
though war arise against me,
yet I will be confident.
⁴One thing have I asked of the
LORD,
that will I seek after:
that I may dwell in the house of
the LORD
all the days of my life,
to gaze upon the beauty of the
LORD
and to inquire in His temple.
⁵For He will hide me in His shelter

in the day of trouble;
He will conceal me under the
cover of His tent;
He will lift me high upon a
rock.
⁶And now my head shall be
lifted up
above my enemies all
around me,
and I will offer in His tent
sacrifices with shouts of joy;
I will sing and make melody to the
Lord.
⁷Hear, O Lord, when I cry aloud;
be gracious to me and answer
me!
⁸You have said, "Seek My face."
My heart says to You,
"Your face, Lord, do I seek."
⁹Hide not Your face from me.
Turn not Your servant away in
anger,
O You who have been my help.
Cast me not off; forsake me not,
O God of my salvation!
¹⁰For my father and my mother
have forsaken me,

but the LORD will take me in.
¹¹Teach me Your way, O LORD,
and lead me on a level path
because of my enemies.
¹²Give me not up to the will of my
adversaries;
for false witnesses have risen
against me,
and they breathe out violence.
¹³I believe that I shall look upon
the goodness of the LORD
in the land of the living!
¹⁴Wait for the LORD;
be strong, and let your heart
take courage;
wait for the LORD!

Blessed is the one whose
transgression is forgiven,
whose sin is covered.
2Blessed is the man against whom
the LORD counts no iniquity,
and in whose spirit there is no
deceit.
3For when I kept silent, my bones
wasted away
through my groaning all day
long.
4For day and night Your hand was
heavy upon me;
my strength was dried up as by
the heat of summer.   *Selah*

5I acknowledged my sin to You,
and I did not cover my iniquity;
I said, "I will confess my
transgressions to the LORD,"
and You forgave the iniquity of
my sin.   *Selah*

6Therefore let everyone who is
godly
offer prayer to You at a time

when You may be found;
surely in the rush of great waters,
they shall not reach him.
⁷You are a hiding place for me;
You preserve me from trouble;
You surround me with shouts
of deliverance.   *Selah*

⁸I will instruct you and teach you
in the way you should go;
I will counsel you
with My eye upon you.
⁹Be not like a horse or a mule,
without understanding,
which must be curbed with bit
and bridle,
or it will not stay near you.
¹⁰Many are the sorrows of the
wicked,
but steadfast love surrounds the
one who trusts in the LORD.
¹¹Be glad in the LORD, and rejoice,
O righteous,
and shout for joy, all you
upright in heart!

God is our refuge and strength,
a very present help in trouble.
²Therefore we will not fear though
the earth gives way,
though the mountains be moved
into the heart of the sea,
³though its waters roar and foam,
though the mountains tremble
at its swelling.   *Selah*
⁴There is a river whose streams
make glad the city of God,
the holy habitation of the Most
High.
⁵God is in the midst of her; she
shall not be moved;
God will help her when
morning dawns.
⁶The nations rage, the kingdoms
totter;
He utters His voice, the earth
melts.
⁷The LORD of hosts is with us;
the God of Jacob is our
fortress.   *Selah*

⁸Come, behold the works of the
Lᴏʀᴅ,
how He has brought desolations
on the earth.
⁹He makes wars cease to the end of
the earth;
He breaks the bow and shatters
the spear;
He burns the chariots with fire.
¹⁰"Be still, and know that I am God.
I will be exalted among the
nations,
I will be exalted in the earth!"
¹¹The Lᴏʀᴅ of hosts is with us;
the God of Jacob is our fortress.

Selah

Have mercy on me, O God,
according to Your steadfast love;
according to Your abundant
mercy
blot out my transgressions.
2Wash me thoroughly from my
iniquity,
and cleanse me from my sin!
3For I know my transgressions,
and my sin is ever before me.
4Against You, You only, have I
sinned
and done what is evil in Your
sight,
so that You may be justified in
Your words
and blameless in Your judgment.
5Behold, I was brought forth in
iniquity,
and in sin did my mother
conceive me.
6Behold, You delight in truth in
the inward being,
and You teach me wisdom in
the secret heart.

⁷Purge me with hyssop, and I shall be clean;
wash me, and I shall be whiter than snow.
⁸Let me hear joy and gladness;
let the bones that You have broken rejoice.
⁹Hide Your face from my sins,
and blot out all my iniquities.
¹⁰Create in me a clean heart, O God,
and renew a right spirit within me.
¹¹Cast me not away from Your presence,
and take not Your Holy Spirit from me.
¹²Restore to me the joy of Your salvation,
and uphold me with a willing spirit.
¹³Then I will teach transgressors Your ways,
and sinners will return to You.
¹⁴Deliver me from bloodguiltiness, O God,
O God of my salvation,

and my tongue will sing aloud
of Your righteousness.
¹⁵O Lord, open my lips,
and my mouth will declare Your
praise.
¹⁶For You will not delight in
sacrifice, or I would give it;
You will not be pleased with a
burnt offering.
¹⁷The sacrifices of God are a broken
spirit;
a broken and contrite heart, O God,
You will not despise.
¹⁸Do good to Zion in Your good
pleasure;
build up the walls of Jerusalem;
¹⁹then will You delight in right
sacrifices,
in burnt offerings and whole
burnt offerings;
then bulls will be offered on
Your altar.

Make a joyful noise to the
LORD, all the earth!
2Serve the LORD with gladness!
Come into His presence with
singing!
3Know that the LORD, He is God!
It is He who made us, and we
are His;
we are His people, and the
sheep of His pasture.
4Enter His gates with thanksgiving,
and His courts with praise!
Give thanks to Him; bless His
name!
5For the LORD is good;
His steadfast love endures
forever,
and His faithfulness to all
generations.

I lift up my eyes to the
hills.
From where does my help
come?
2My help comes from the LORD,
who made heaven and earth.
3He will not let your foot be
moved;
He who keeps you will not
slumber.
4Behold, He who keeps Israel
will neither slumber nor sleep.
5The LORD is your keeper;
the LORD is your shade on
your right hand.
6The sun shall not strike you
by day,
nor the moon by night.
7The LORD will keep you from all
evil;
He will keep your life.
8The LORD will keep
your going out and your
coming in
from this time forth and
forevermore.

Unless the LORD builds the house,
those who build it labor in vain.
Unless the LORD watches over the
city,
the watchman stays awake in
vain.
²It is in vain that you rise up early
and go late to rest,
eating the bread of anxious toil;
for He gives to His beloved
sleep.
³Behold, children are a heritage
from the LORD,
the fruit of the womb a reward.
⁴Like arrows in the hand of a
warrior
are the children of one's youth.
⁵Blessed is the man
who fills his quiver with them!
He shall not be put to shame
when he speaks with his
enemies in the gate.

Hear my prayer, O LORD;
give ear to my pleas for mercy!
In your faithfulness answer me,
in Your righteousness!
²Enter not into judgment with Your
servant,
for no one living is righteous
before You.
³For the enemy has pursued my
soul;
he has crushed my life to the
ground;
he has made me sit in darkness
like those long dead.
⁴Therefore my spirit faints within
me;
my heart within me is appalled.
⁵I remember the days of old;
I meditate on all that You have
done;
I ponder the work of Your
hands.
⁶I stretch out my hands to You;
my soul thirsts for You like a
parched land.   *Selah*

7Answer me quickly, O Lord!
My spirit fails!
Hide not Your face from me,
lest I be like those who go down
to the pit.
8Let me hear in the morning of
Your steadfast love,
for in You I trust.
Make me know the way I
should go,
for to You I lift up my soul.
9Deliver me from my enemies,
O Lord!
I have fled to You for refuge!
10Teach me to do Your will,
for You are my God!
Let Your good Spirit lead me
on level ground!
11For Your name's sake, O Lord,
preserve my life!
In Your righteousness bring my
soul out of trouble!
12And in Your steadfast love You will
cut off my enemies,
and You will destroy all the
adversaries of my soul,
for I am Your servant.

Praise the LORD!
Praise the LORD from the
heavens;
praise Him in the heights!
²Praise Him, all His angels;
praise Him, all His hosts!
³Praise Him, sun and moon,
praise Him, all you shining stars!
⁴Praise Him, you highest heavens,
and you waters above the
heavens!
⁵ Let them praise the name
of the LORD!
For He commanded and they
were created.
⁶And He established them forever
and ever;
He gave a decree, and it shall
not pass away.
⁷Praise the LORD from the earth,
you great sea creatures and all
deeps,
⁸ fire and hail, snow and mist,
stormy wind fulfilling His word!
⁹ Mountains and all hills,

fruit trees and all cedars!
¹⁰ Beasts and all livestock,
creeping things and flying
birds!
¹¹Kings of the earth and all
peoples,
princes and all rulers of the
earth!
¹²Young men and maidens
together,
old men and children!
¹³ Let them praise the name
of the LORD,
for His name alone is exalted;
His majesty is above earth and
heaven.
¹⁴He has raised up a horn for His
people,
praise for all His saints,
for the people of Israel who are
near to Him.
Praise the LORD!

Praise the LORD!
Praise God in His sanctuary;
praise Him in His mighty
heavens!
²Praise Him for His mighty deeds;
praise Him according to His
excellent greatness!
³Praise Him with trumpet sound;
praise Him with lute and harp!
⁴Praise Him with tambourine and
dance;
praise Him with strings and
pipe!
⁵Praise Him with sounding
cymbals;
praise Him with loud clashing
cymbals!
⁶Let everything that has breath
praise the LORD!
Praise the LORD!

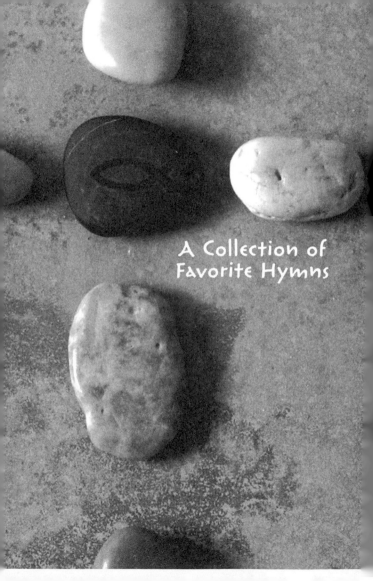

A Collection of
Favorite Hymns

Now the Light Has Gone Away

Now the light has gone away;
Father, listen while I pray,
Asking Thee to watch and keep
And to send me quiet sleep.

Jesus, Savior, wash away
All that has been wrong today;
Help me ev'ry day to be
Good and gentle, more like Thee.

Let my near and dear ones be
Always near and dear to Thee;
Oh, bring me and all I love
To Thy happy home above.

Now my evening praise I give;
Thou didst die that I might live.
All my blessings come from Thee;
Oh, how good Thou art to me!

Thou, my best and kindest Friend,
Thou wilt love me to the end.
Let me love Thee more and more,
Always better than before. Amen. (*TLH* 653)

—Frances Havergal

Go, My children, with My blessing,
Never alone.
Waking, sleeping, I am with you;
You are My own.
In My love's baptismal river I have made you
Mine forever.
Go, My children, with My blessing—
You are My own.

Go, My children, sins forgiven,
At peace and pure.
Here you learned how much I love you,
What I can cure.
Here you heard My dear Son's story;
Here you touched Him, saw His glory.
Go, My children, sins forgiven,
At peace and pure.

Go, My children, fed and nourished,
Closer to Me;
Grow in love and love by serving,
Joyful and free.
Here My Spirit's power filled you;
Here His tender comfort stilled you.
Go, My children, fed and nourished,
Joyful and free.

I the Lord will bless and keep you
And give you peace;
I the Lord will smile upon you
And give you peace;
I the Lord will be your Father, Savior,
Comforter, and Brother.
Go, My children; I will keep you
And give you peace. (*LSB* 922)

—Jaroslav Vajda

Abide with Me

Abide with me, fast falls the eventide.
The darkness deepens; Lord, with me abide.
When other helpers fail and comforts flee,
Help of the helpless, O abide with me.

I need Thy presence ev'ry passing hour;
What but Thy grace can foil the tempter's
pow'r?
Who like Thyself my guide and stay can be?
Through cloud and sunshine, O abide with me.

Come not in terrors, as the King of kings,
But kind and good, with healing in Thy
wings;
Tears for all woes, a heart for ev'ry plea.
Come, Friend of sinners, thus abide with me.

Swift to its close ebbs out life's little day;
Earth's joys grow dim, its glories pass away;
Change and decay in all around I see;
O Thou who changest not, abide with me.

I fear no foe with Thee at hand to bless;
Ills have no weight and tears no bitterness.
Where is death's sting? Where, grave, thy
victory?
I triumph still if Thou abide with me!

Hold Thou Thy cross before my closing eyes;
Shine through the gloom, and point me to the skies.
Heav'n's morning breaks, and earth's vain shadows flee;
In life, in death, O Lord, abide with me.
(*LSB* 878)

—Henry F. Lyte

Praise to the Lord, the Almighty, the King of
creation!
O my soul, praise Him, for He is your health
and salvation!
　　Let all who hear
　　Now to His temple draw near,
Joining in glad adoration!

Praise to the Lord, who o'er all things is
wondrously reigning
And, as on wings of an eagle, uplifting,
sustaining.
　　Have you not seen
　　All that is needful has been
Sent by His gracious ordaining?

Praise to the Lord, who has fearfully,
wondrously, made you,
Health has bestowed and, when heedlessly
falling, has stayed you.
　　What need or grief
　　Ever has failed of relief?
Wings of His mercy did shade you.

Praise to the Lord, who will prosper your work
and defend you;

Surely His goodness and mercy shall daily
attend you.
Ponder anew
What the Almighty can do
As with His love He befriends you.

Praise to the Lord! O let all that is in me adore
Him!
All that has life and breath, come now with
praises before Him!
Let the Amen
Sound from His people again;
Gladly forever adore Him! (*LSB* 790)

—Joachim Neander

I Know That My Redeemer Lives

I know that my Redeemer lives;
What comfort this sweet sentence gives!
He lives, He lives, who once was dead;
He lives, my ever-living head.

He lives triumphant from the grave;
He lives eternally to save;
He lives all-glorious in the sky;
He lives exalted there on high.

He lives to bless me with His love;
He lives to plead for me above;
He lives my hungry soul to feed;
He lives to help in time of need.

He lives to grant me rich supply;
He lives to guide me with His eye;
He lives to comfort me when faint;
He lives to hear my soul's complaint.

He lives to silence all my fears;
He lives to wipe away my tears;
He lives to calm my troubled heart;
He lives all blessings to impart.

He lives, my kind, wise, heav'nly friend;
He lives and loves me to the end;
He lives, and while He lives, I'll sing;
He lives, my Prophet, Priest, and King.

He lives and grants me daily breath;
He lives, and I shall conquer death;
He lives my mansion to prepare;
He lives to bring me safely there.

He lives, all glory to His name!
He lives, my Jesus, still the same;
Oh, the sweet joy this sentence gives:
I know that my Redeemer lives! (*LSB* 461)

—Samuel Medley

Praise God,
from Whom All Blessings Flow
(The Doxology)

Praise God, from whom all blessings flow;
Praise Him, all creatures here below;
Praise Him above, ye heav'nly host:
Praise Father, Son, and Holy Ghost.
  Amen. (*LSB* 805)

—Thomas Ken

Beautiful Savior

Beautiful Savior, King of creation,
Son of God and Son of Man!
    Truly I'd love Thee,
    Truly I'd serve Thee,
Light of my soul, my joy, my crown.

Fair are the meadows, Fair are the woodlands,
Robed in flow'rs of blooming spring;
    Jesus is fairer,
    Jesus is purer,
He makes our sorr'wing spirit sing.

Fair is the sunshine, Fair is the moonlight,
Bright the sparkling stars on high;
    Jesus shines brighter,
    Jesus shines purer
Than all the angels in the sky.

Beautiful Savior, Lord of the nations,
Son of God and Son of Man!
    Glory and honor,
    Praise, adoration
Now and forevermore be Thine! (*LSB* 537)

—*Münsterisch Gesangbuch*

For All the Saints

For all the saints who from their labors rest,
Who Thee by faith before the world confessed,
Thy name, O Jesus, be forever blest.
    Alleluia! Alleluia!

Thou wast their rock, their fortress, and their
might;
Thou, Lord, their captain in the well-fought
fight;
Thou, in the darkness drear, their one true
light.
    Alleluia! Alleluia!

Oh, may Thy soldiers, faithful, true, and bold,
Fight as the saints who nobly fought of old
And win with them the victor's crown of gold!
    Alleluia! Alleluia!

Oh, blest communion, fellowship divine!
We feebly struggle, they in glory shine;
Yet all are one in Thee, for all are Thine.
    Alleluia! Alleluia!

And when the fight is fierce, the warfare long,
Steals on the ear the distant triumph song,
And hearts are brave again, and arms are
strong.
  Alleluia! Alleluia!

The golden evening brightens in the west;
Soon, soon to faithful warriors cometh rest;
Sweet is the calm of paradise the blest.
  Alleluia! Alleluia!

But, lo, there breaks a yet more glorious day:
The saints triumphant rise in bright array;
The King of Glory passes on His way.
  Alleluia! Alleluia!

From earth's wide bounds, from ocean's
farthest coast,
Through gates of pearl streams in the
countless host,
Singing to Father, Son, and Holy Ghost:
  Alleluia! Alleluia! (*LSB* 677)

—William W. How

Be Still, My Soul

Be still, my soul; the Lord is on your side;
   Bear patiently the cross of grief or pain;
Leave to your God to order and provide;
   In ev'ry change He faithful will remain.
Be still, my soul; your best, your heav'nly
Friend
Through thorny ways leads to a joyful end.

Be still, my soul; your God will undertake
   To guide the future as He has the past.
Your hope, your confidence let nothing shake;
   All now mysterious shall be bright at last.
Be still, my soul; the waves and winds still
know
His voice who ruled them while He dwelt
below.

Be still, my soul; though dearest friends depart
   And all is darkened in this vale of tears;
Then you will better know His love, His heart,
   Who comes to soothe your sorrows and
   your fears.
Be still, my soul; your Jesus can repay
From His own fullness all He takes away.

Be still, my soul; the hour is hast'ning on
 When we shall be forever with the Lord,
When disappointment, grief, and fear are
gone,
 Sorrow forgot, love's purest joys restored.
Be still, my soul; when change and tears are
past,
All safe and blessed we shall meet at last.
(*LSB* 752)

—Catharina Amalia Dorothea von Schlegel

Thy strong word did cleave the darkness;
  At Thy speaking it was done.
For created light we thank Thee,
  While Thine ordered seasons run.
Alleluia, alleluia!
  Praise to Thee who light dost send!
Alleluia, alleluia!
  Alleluia without end!

Lo, on those who dwelt in darkness,
  Dark as night and deep as death,
Broke the light of Thy salvation,
  Breathed Thine own life-breathing breath.
Alleluia, alleluia!
  Praise to Thee who light dost send!
Alleluia, alleluia!
  Alleluia without end!

Thy strong Word bespeaks us righteous;
  Bright with Thine own holiness,
Glorious now, we press toward glory,
  And our lives our hopes confess.
Alleluia, alleluia!
  Praise to Thee who light dost send!
Alleluia, alleluia!
  Alleluia without end!

From the cross Thy wisdom shining
    Breaketh forth in conqu'ring might;
From the cross forever beameth
    All Thy bright redeeming light.
Alleluia, alleluia!
    Praise to Thee who light dost send!
Alleluia, alleluia!
    Alleluia without end!

Give us lips to sing Thy glory,
    Tongues Thy mercy to proclaim,
Throats that shout the hope that fills us,
    Mouths to speak Thy holy name.
Alleluia, alleluia!
    May the light which Thou dost send
Fill our songs with alleluias,
    Alleluias without end!

God the Father, light-creator,
    To Thee laud and honor be.
To Thee, Light of Light begotten,
    Praise be sung eternally.
Holy Spirit, light-revealer,
    Glory, glory be to Thee.
Mortals, angels, now and ever
    Praise the holy Trinity! (*LSB* 578)

—Martin H. Franzmann

Hark, the voice of Jesus calling,
   "Who will go and work today?
Fields are white and harvests waiting—
   Who will bear the sheaves away?"
Loud and long the Master calleth;
   Rich reward He offers thee.
Who will answer, gladly saying,
   "Here am I, send me, send me"?

Some take up His task in morning,
   To their Lord responding soon;
Some are called in heat of midday,
   Others late in afternoon;
Even as the sun is setting,
   Some are sent into the fields,
There to gather in the bounty
   That God's Word so richly yields.

For as rain and snow from heaven
   Water seeds in dusty soil,
Causing them to bud and flower,
   Giving bread to those who toil;
So the Lord sends forth His promise,
   Words of life and joy and peace—
Never void to Him returning,
   Bearing fruit with great increase.

Hearken to the Lord whose coming
    Marks the time when grace shall end,
When with His angelic reapers
    He in glory shall descend.
Soon the night, the final harvest;
    Soon the time for work shall cease.
Then the souls His grace has garnered
    Shall enjoy His Sabbath peace. (*LSB* 827)

—Daniel March

Stz 2–4 © 2001 Stephen P. Starke
Admin. by Concordia Publishing House.

My Hope Is Built on Nothing Less

My hope is built on nothing less
Than Jesus' blood and righteousness;
No merit of my own I claim
But wholly lean on Jesus' name.
On Christ, the solid rock, I stand;
All other ground is sinking sand.

When darkness veils His lovely face,
I rest on His unchanging grace;
In ev'ry high and stormy gale
My anchor holds within the veil.
On Christ, the solid rock, I stand;
All other ground is sinking sand.

His oath, His covenant and blood
Support me in the raging flood;
When ev'ry earthly prop gives way,
He then is all my hope and stay.
On Christ, the solid rock, I stand;
All other ground is sinking sand.

When He shall come with trumpet sound,
Oh, may I then in Him be found,
Clothed in His righteousness alone,
Redeemed to stand before His throne!
On Christ, the solid rock, I stand;
All other ground is sinking sand.
(*LSB* 575/576)

—Edward Mote

My Song Is Love Unknown

My song is love unknown,
   My Savior's love to me,
Love to the loveless shown
   That they might lovely be.
Oh, who am I
   That for my sake
   My Lord should take
Frail flesh and die?

He came from His blest throne
   Salvation to bestow;
But men made strange, and none
   The longed-for Christ would know.
But, oh, my friend,
   My friend indeed,
   Who at my need
His life did spend!

Sometimes they strew His way
   And His sweet praises sing;
Resounding all the day
   Hosannas to their King.
Then "Crucify!"
   Is all their breath,
   And for His death
They thirst and cry.

Why, what hath my Lord done?
    What makes this rage and spite?
He made the lame to run,
    He gave the blind their sight.
Sweet injuries!
    Yet they at these
    Themselves displease
And 'gainst Him rise.

They rise and needs will have
    My dear Lord made away;
A murderer they save,
    The Prince of Life they slay.
Yet cheerful He
    To suff'ring goes
    That He His foes
From thence might free.

In life no house, no home
    My Lord on earth might have;
In death no friendly tomb
    But what a stranger gave.
What may I say?
    Heav'n was His home
    But mine the tomb
Wherein He lay.

Here might I stay and sing,
   No story so divine!
Never was love, dear King,
   Never was grief like Thine.
This is my friend,
   In whose sweet praise
   I all my days
Could gladly spend! (*LSB* 430)

—Samuel Crossman

Take my life and let it be
Consecrated, Lord, to Thee;
Take my moments and my days,
Let them flow in ceaseless praise.

Take my hands and let them move
At the impulse of Thy love;
Take my feet and let them be
Swift and beautiful for Thee.

Take my voice and let me sing
Always, only for my King;
Take my lips and let them be
Filled with messages from Thee.

Take my silver and my gold,
Not a mite would I withhold;
Take my intellect and use
Ev'ry pow'r as Thou shalt choose.

Take my will and make it Thine,
It shall be no longer mine;
Take my heart, it is Thine own,
It shall be Thy royal throne.

Take my love, my Lord, I pour
At Thy feet its treasure store;
Take myself, and I will be
Ever, only, all for Thee. (*LSB* 783)

—Frances R. Havergal

I'm But a Stranger Here

I'm but a stranger here,
Heav'n is my home;
Earth is a desert drear,
Heav'n is my home.
Danger and sorrow stand
Round me on ev'ry hand;
Heav'n is my fatherland,
Heav'n is my home.

What though the tempest rage,
Heav'n is my home;
Short is my pilgrimage,
Heav'n is my home;
And time's wild wintry blast
Soon shall be overpast;
I shall reach home at last,
Heav'n is my home.

Therefore I murmur not,
Heav'n is my home;
Whate'er my earthly lot,
Heav'n is my home;
And I shall surely stand
There at my Lord's right hand;
Heav'n is my fatherland,
Heav'n is my home. (*LSB* 748)

—Thomas R. Taylor

At the Lamb's high feast we sing
Praise to our victorious King,
Who has washed us in the tide
Flowing from His piercèd side.
    Alleluia!

Praise we Him, whose love divine
Gives His sacred blood for wine,
Gives His body for the feast—
Christ the victim, Christ the priest.
    Alleluia!

Where the paschal blood is poured,
Death's dread angel sheathes the sword;
Israel's hosts triumphant go
Through the wave that drowns the foe.
    Alleluia!

Praise we Christ, whose blood was shed,
Paschal victim, paschal bread;
With sincerity and love
Eat we manna from above.
    Alleluia!

Mighty Victim from the sky,
Hell's fierce pow'rs beneath You lie;
You have conquered in the fight,
You have brought us life and light.
    Alleluia!

Now no more can death appall,
Now no more the grave enthrall;
You have opened paradise,
And Your saints in You shall rise.
    Alleluia!

Easter triumph, Easter joy!
This alone can sin destroy;
From sin's pow'r, Lord, set us free,
Newborn souls in You to be.
    Alleluia!

Father, who the crown shall give,
Savior, by whose death we live,
Spirit, guide through all our days:
Three in One, Your name we praise.
    Alleluia! (*LSB* 633)

                            —Robert Campbell, translator

Joyful, Joyful We Adore Thee

Joyful, joyful we adore Thee,
    God of glory, Lord of love!
Hearts unfold like flow'rs before Thee,
    Praising Thee, their sun above.
Melt the clouds of sin and sadness,
    Drive the gloom of doubt away.
Giver of immortal gladness,
    Fill us with the light of day.

All Thy works with joy surround Thee,
    Earth and heav'n reflect Thy rays,
Stars and angels sing around Thee,
    Center of unbroken praise.
Field and forest, vale and mountain,
    Flow'ry meadow, flashing sea,
Chanting bird, and flowing fountain
    Call us to rejoice in Thee.

Thou art giving and forgiving,
    Ever blessing, ever blest,
Wellspring of the joy of living,
    Ocean-depth of happy rest!
Father, Son, and Holy Spirit,
    Fountainhead of love divine:
Joyful, we Thy heav'n inherit!
    Joyful, we by grace are Thine! (*LSB* 803)

—Henry Van Dyke

The Lamb

The Lamb, the Lamb,
O Father, where's the sacrifice?
    Faith sees, believes
God will provide the Lamb of price! *Refrain*

Refrain (after each stanza):
Worthy is the Lamb whose death makes me
His own!
The Lamb is reigning on His throne!

The Lamb, the Lamb,
One perfect final offering.
    The Lamb, the Lamb,
Let earth join heav'n His praise to sing.
Refrain

The Lamb, the Lamb,
As wayward sheep their shepherd kill
    So still, His will
On our behalf the Law to fill.
Refrain

He sighs, He dies,
He takes my sin and wretchedness.
    He lives, forgives,
He gives me His own righteousness. *Refrain*

He rose, He rose,
My heart with thanks now overflows.
    His song prolong
Till ev'ry heart to Him belong.
Refrain (*LSB* 547)

—Gerald P. Coleman

Christ Be My Leader

Christ be my Leader by night as by day;
Safe through the darkness, for He is the way.
Gladly I follow, my future His care,
Darkness is daylight when Jesus is there.

Christ be my Teacher in age as in youth,
Drifting or doubting, for He is the truth.
Grant me to trust Him; though shifting
as sand,
Doubt cannot daunt me; in Jesus I stand.

Christ be my Savior in calm as in strife;
Death cannot hold me, for He is the life.
Nor darkness nor doubting nor sin and
its stain
Can touch my salvation: with Jesus I reign.
(*LSB* 861)

—Timothy Dudley-Smith

Earth and all stars!
  Loud rushing planets!
Sing to the Lord a new song!
  Oh, victory!
  Loud shouting army!
Sing to the Lord a new song!

Refrain:
He has done marvelous things.
I too will praise Him with a new song!

Hail, wind, and rain!
  Loud blowing snowstorm!
Sing to the Lord a new song!
  Flowers and trees!
  Loud rustling dry leaves!
Sing to the Lord a new song! *Refrain*

Trumpet and pipes!
  Loud clashing cymbals!
Sing to the Lord a new song!
  Harp, lute, and lyre!
  Loud humming cellos!
Sing to the Lord a new song! *Refrain*

Engines and steel!
  Loud pounding hammers!

Sing to the Lord a new song!
  Limestone and beams!
  Loud building workers!
Sing to the Lord a new song! *Refrain*

Classrooms and labs!
  Loud boiling test tubes!
Sing to the Lord a new song!
  Athlete and band!
  Loud cheering people!
Sing to the Lord a new song! *Refrain*

Knowledge and truth!
  Loud sounding wisdom!
Sing to the Lord a new song!
  Daughter and son!
  Loud praying members!
Sing to the Lord a new song! *Refrain*

Children of God,
  Dying and rising,
Sing to the Lord a new song!
  Heaven and earth,
  Hosts everlasting,
Sing to the Lord a new song! *Refrain*
(*LSB* 817)

—Herbert F. Brokering

Lift High the Cross

Lift high the cross, the love of Christ proclaim
Till all the world adore His sacred name.

Come, Christians, follow where our
Captain trod,
Our king victorious, Christ, the Son
of God. *Refrain*

Led on their way by this triumphant sign,
The hosts of God in conquering ranks
combine. *Refrain*

All newborn soldiers of the Crucified
Bear on their brows the seal of Him who died.
Refrain

O Lord, once lifted on the glorious tree,
As Thou hast promised, draw us all to Thee.
Refrain

Let every race and every language tell
Of Him who saves our lives from death and
hell. *Refrain*

So shall our song of triumph ever be:
Praise to the Crucified for victory! *Refrain*
(*LSB* 837)

—George W. Kitchin & Michael R. Newbolt
Copyright © 1974 Hope Publishing Co.

A Mighty Fortress Is Our God

A mighty fortress is our God,
    A trusty shield and weapon;
He helps us free from ev'ry need
    That hath us now o'ertaken.
The old evil foe
Now means deadly woe;
    Deep guile and great might
    Are his dread arms in fight;
On earth is not his equal.

With might of ours can naught be done,
    Soon were our loss effected;
But for us fights the valiant One,
    Whom God Himself elected.
Ask ye, Who is this?
Jesus Christ it is,
    Of Sabaoth Lord,
    And there's none other God;
He holds the field forever.

Though devils all the world should fill,
    All eager to devour us,
We tremble not, we fear no ill;
    They shall not overpow'r us.
This world's prince may still
Scowl fierce as he will,

He can harm us none.
He's judged; the deed is done;
One little word can fell him.

The Word they still shall let remain
    Nor any thanks have for it;
He's by our side upon the plain
    With His good gifts and Spirit.
And take they our life,
Goods, fame, child, and wife,
    Though these all be gone,
    Our vict'ry has been won;
The Kingdom ours remaineth. (*LSB* 656)

—Martin Luther

Come, Thou Fount of Every Blessing

Come, Thou Fount of ev'ry blessing,
　　Tune my heart to sing Thy grace;
Streams of mercy, never ceasing,
　　Call for songs of loudest praise.
While the hope of endless glory
　　Fills my heart with joy and love,
Teach me ever to adore Thee;
　　May I still Thy goodness prove.

Here I raise my Ebenezer,
　　Hither by Thy help I've come;
And I hope, by Thy good pleasure,
　　Safely to arrive at home.
Jesus sought me when a stranger,
　　Wand'ring from the fold of God;
He, to rescue me from danger,
　　Interposed His precious blood.

Oh, to grace how great a debtor
　　Daily I'm constrained to be;
Let that grace now like a fetter
　　Bind my wand'ring heart to Thee:
Prone to wander, Lord, I feel it;
　　Prone to leave the God I love.
Here's my heart, O take and seal it,
　　Seal it for Thy courts above.

Oh, that day when freed from sinning,
    I shall see Thy lovely face;
Clothed then in the blood-washed linen,
    How I'll sing Thy wondrous grace!
Come, my Lord, no longer tarry;
    Take my ransom'd soul away;
Send Thine angels soon to carry
    Me to realms of endless day. (*LSB* 686)

—Robert Robinson

© Shutterstock.com/Julie Hagan

A Thought for Today
Devotions for special days throughout the year

My Birthday

"How many are the days of the years of your life?" Genesis 47:8

Birthdays are a time for reflection and resolution.

Repentant reflection and rededication mean that we look at our dying years in terms of the many blessings God has sent, in particular our new birth, which God gave us through Holy Baptism.

But mingled with these memories of His mercy are also memories of our mistakes, "Thy grace abused, my misspent years." How often have we forgotten that He is the only source of our years!

That is why a birthday is a time for rededication. For the sake of Christ, the Holy Spirit comes into our hearts that the year, begun with this birthday, may be a year fully dedicated to God.

—Jaroslav Pelikan Jr.

Unfailing Love

....

"You will abide in My love." John 15:10

"If you keep My commandments, you will abide in My love," the Savior said. In the year now past, we found His promise true. We enter this new year unafraid. Anchored in the Father's love and in the love of the Son, who gave us His life, this promise must remain true. But "greater love has no one than this, that someone lays down his life for his friends" (John 15:13). This love is the key to the Father's heart. Whatever we ask the Father in the name of His Son, He will give us.

Heavenly Father, forgive us our sins of the past year and keep us in the love of Your Son. Amen.

—Lewis Spitz

New Year's Day

Forward
. . . .

"Tell the people . . . to go forward." Exodus 14:15

"Go forward," Moses told Israel, afraid of Pharaoh's mighty hosts. Was God demanding the impossible? Indeed not! He "made the sea dry land" (Exodus 14:21).

"Go forward," God commands us today. By grace He brought us to Christ. In Jesus we have forgiveness. We are His people. But we face enormous difficulties and temptations. Yet God says: Go!

"Go forward" is God's command in our Church in this new year. But the world's condition frightens us. Can we go forward? Indeed! God gave Christ "as head over all things to the church" (Ephesians 1:22). He will defeat all our enemies.

—John Behnken

Christmas Joy

"Behold, I bring you good news of a great joy."
Luke 2:10

Christmas joy is the greatest joy on earth. All others have their limits. Harvest joys are modified by the remembrance of hail and drought; victory joys are tempered by the sadness of the defeated and the mourning for the dead. Here is victory without regret. The Child of Bethlehem has defeated the powers of darkness that held mankind in bondage. The fruit of His victory no hail, no sun, no flood can spoil. It brings healing to the sin-stricken heart. Christmas joy enters any home—to make the poor rich and the wealthy richer; to open the eyes of the sick and dying to the joys of heaven. Thank God for the joy of Christmas!

—Theodore Hoyer

Epiphany

Seeing

"We saw His star when it rose and have come to worship Him." Matthew 2:2

The Wise Men had seen His star. With eyes of faith they now saw the glory of the new-born King. They looked beyond all lowliness and unbelief. They knew that the King had appeared who would bring blessings to mankind. They firmly believed that this newborn King would bring deliverance from the foes that have enslaved mankind since Adam's fall. Him they must worship.

I, too, must hasten to Bethlehem, for there is my King, who has freed me from every sin, my fear of death, and Satan's power. I, too, have seen His star, and I have come to worship Him.

—Fred Mayer

Faithful

"Be faithful unto death." Revelation 2:10

Kneeling in humble consecration at Jesus' altar, trusting only in His merit for salvation, taking upon oneself His yoke, suffering tribulation and shame for His name—all this belongs to the Christian profession and will find its reward if the bond of loyalty is found unsevered at life's end.

The athlete collapsing near the goal, the army running out of ammunition with victory in sight, each shows that "almost" is not enough. Completion crowns the work. Through Christ's perfect life and His suffering, death, and resurrection, our victory is assured. The crown of life is ours.

—Otto Sohn

Monday of Holy Week

Go Away?

....

"Lord, to whom shall we go?" John 6:68

People are disappointed in Jesus, not because of what Jesus is but because of what they are. Many go away from Jesus to worship at the altars of materialism, imagining that man lives by bread alone.

Shall we also go away? Peter dreaded the very thought. So do all believers.

Go away from Jesus? None other can be what Jesus is: the God-man, able to save sinners. None other can remove from us the ugly blotches of our sins. None other loves us as Jesus loves us. None other can give us the peace and joy that Jesus gives. Lord Jesus, we will follow Thee in love.

—Robert Lange

Tuesday of Holy Week

Paradise
....

"Today you will be with Me in Paradise."
Luke 23:43

To the dying thief, Jesus gave a promise greater than he dared hope for, the promise of heaven.

Jesus had come to save sinners. He was in the act of giving His life for fallen man. What was more fitting than that, from His cross, He should make this promise to a sinner who looked to Him in faith? To be with Jesus in paradise—that is the supreme happiness. Who could hope for more?

Here is a promise full of comfort and hope. It sweetens the sometimes bitter cup of life. It gives hope in the face of death. In life and death it assures the Christian that the best is yet to be.

—Felix Kretzschmar

Forsaken

....

"My God, My God, why have You forsaken Me?" Mark 15:34

Our Savior's anguished cry marks the climax of His Passion. After hours of grievous physical pain, He stood before the majestic Judge who sentenced Him to suffer the agony of eternal death.

The Judge was His Father who had sent Him. As the sinner's substitute, the Son willingly assumed the guilt and punishment of our race. Jesus, the Sin-bearer, groaned as He drank the cup of wrath and His innocent soul was enveloped by the horrors of damnation.

In that dark hour, justice was satisfied. Because our Mediator was forsaken, the Father's heart and house are open to us all.

–Carl Hoffmann

Furnished

....

"He will show you a large upper room furnished." Luke 22:12

We go to great lengths to make our homes comfortable. We plan carefully and spend wisely. Everything must have a definite purpose. Our efforts at comfort and serviceability cannot compare with God's. We concern ourselves with the body; God concentrates on the soul. His love for us led His Son to the cross, where He died to furnish an upper room in heaven for us all. That love does not leave us alone. It draws us into the upper room. There we see God in His majesty and beauty, surrounded by the angels and saints, who sing and praise His mercy. Gone are worry, tears, and fears. There, satisfaction supreme is ours through Christ.

—Alex William C. Guebert

Good Friday

Words
....

"And when they had crucified Him . . ."
Matthew 27:35

A wealth of theology is deposited in the words of this text. The word *crucified* marks the climax of a divine life that was dedicated to the welfare of man. The *and* includes the other acts of disobedience that preceded the crucifixion: the betrayal, the unjust trial, a night of chastisement.

The pronouns *they* and *Him* are the key to the text. *They* who deserved crucifixion nailed to the cross *Him* who was divinely innocent. *They* includes me. He died on the cross for me. Cleansed by the blood of the Crucified, I am an heir to His eternal glory. Truly, "in the cross of Christ I glory" (*LSB* 427:1).

—Alfred von Rohr Sauer

Saturday of Holy Week

Made Sin

....

"For our sake He made Him to be sin."
2 Corinthians 5:21

An amazing statement! God made His Son,
Jesus, to be sin. Jesus did not sin. He was holy.
Now God did not make Jesus a sinner; He left
Him as sinless as He was. But He made Him
to be sin for us. He laid upon Him the sins of
the world. Never were so many sins gathered
in one place as on the cross of Calvary. And
among all those sins borne by Jesus were
also my sins. God took them from me and
laid them on Him. My sin was charged to
Christ's account, and Christ's righteousness
was credited to me. Believing this marvelously
comforting truth, I can spend this life in peace
and eternity in heaven.

—A. H. Schwermann

He is Risen!

"He is risen." Matthew 28:6 NKJV

Friends had come to sprinkle sweet spices on a cold corpse and then let the thick walls of the tomb hide from their eyes the decay of life and hope.

So time must bring the day when others will do the futile service of love also for us. For without Easter we are without hope.

Comes Easter Day: "He is not here!" Where the crucified Son of God was laid, there lies buried instead the sting of death. Death itself lies entombed.

"He is risen." Now our dying is not death. Redeemed, cleansed, justified, we take no sin to the grave; raised by the Risen One, we shall be like Him, for we shall see Him as He is. Hallelujah!

—Walter Roehrs

Ascension

The Ascension Vision

"As they were looking on, He was lifted up."
Acts 1:9

What did the friends of Jesus behold until the cloud covered Him? His hands uplifted and nail prints in His palms, witnesses to the evil the world returned for His life of goodness. Yet not to curse are those hands uplifted, but to bless. Blessing removes the curse. For this He had come. Now the Savior enters the eternal world to be crowned Lord of all.

The parting vision of the ascending Lord should always be alive in our hearts. Upon the throne He also is facing us to give forgiveness and salvation.

If we accept this offer, we shall one day see Him with outstretched hands, to bless us evermore.

—Victor Bartling

Pentecost Power

....

"They were all filled with the Holy Spirit."
Acts 2:4

This Scripture passage is the key that unlocks the mysteries of the Christian faith. How did the disciples know that the risen Christ was their Lord and that salvation is in no other? How does Scripture account for their fearless witness, their brotherly love, and their readiness to die for Jesus? "They were all filled with the Holy Spirit."

This Pentecost miracle is repeated today whenever someone is baptized into the Christian faith and believes in Christ. That person glorifies Jesus by confessing Him and following Him. Through the Spirit's indwelling, he conquers sin and lives in Christ now and forever.

—Paul Bretscher

Blessed

"Her children rise up and call her blessed."
Proverbs 31:28

One of the finest emotions known among humans is a mother's love. Surpassed only by the unspeakable love of God, her love perseveres through sickness and want, through sorrow and joy, yes, even through transgression and folly.

Such love comes to its full fruit when it directs the hearts and minds of the children to trust in their Savior. The Christian mother's prayer, her daily conversation, and her devout life nurture the young in the fear of the Lord.

We who enjoy this priceless gift of a Christian mother's love will also arise and call her "blessed," for she has been a blessing to us and led us to our blessed Savior.

—Arthur Repp

In Memory

....

*"This is My name forever . . . I am to be
remembered throughout all generations."*
Exodus 3:15

This is our memorial to all generations—
the gravestones and crosses in cemeteries
everywhere. They recall what yesterday's
honored dead gave of love and devotion to
God and country.

"I am to be remembered throughout all
generations," says God. He created a perfect
world for man's heritage and gave His only-
begotten Son as Redeemer of man's sin-lost
heritage. To all who believe in the Redeemer,
He gives pardon and peace and the future
hope of glory.

—Martin Poch

Birthdays

"Let every person be subject to the governing authorities. . . . Those that exist have been instituted by God." Romans 13:1

Today we celebrate the birthday of our nation.

Festivals are reminders of divine blessings. On this day, we think particularly of those blessings that God gave us through the founding fathers, who brought forth a nation established on the principles of political, social, and religious freedom and who gave us a form of government that for generations has safeguarded the fundamental rights of man. All governments are of God though established through men. Good governments are a blessing of God. Today we can resolve to be more faithful as Christian citizens.

—A. M. Rehwinkel

Reformation Day

The Reformation Important

"I saw another angel . . . with an eternal gospel." Revelation 14:6

What makes the Reformation meaningful for *me?* That it changed our world's political, economic, and cultural destiny? That it gave Western Christendom religious services in the language of the people?

These things are important. But more important for *me* is that through the Reformation has been opened to *me* a knowledge of God's will and word. I see clearly my native spiritual helplessness and sinfulness. But I also have the Gospel. And the Gospel gives me counsel, forgiveness, and aid against sin through the spoken Word and the Holy Sacraments. This I owe to the Reformation.

—Arthur Piepkorn

Sing

"Sing to the LORD with thanksgiving."
Psalm 147:7

Wherever the Word of Christ dwells richly in believers, there resound psalms, hymns, and spiritual songs. In heathen lands, such songs of thanksgiving are not known.

But at times we fail to sing to the Lord. Unmindful of God's manifold mercies, our lips are silent. But dare we keep silence?

Divine love continually calls for our grateful songs. The psalmist says that God prepares rain for the earth and fills us with the finest of wheat. He strengthens the bars of our gates and makes peace within our borders. He sends out His Word and heals the broken in heart (see Psalm 147).

Truly, God's amazing mercies must ever move us to sing to Him.

—John Mueller

A Collection of Prayers

Morning

Faithful God, whose mercies are new to us every morning, we humbly pray that You would look upon us in mercy and renew us by Your Holy Spirit. Keep safe our going out and our coming in, and let Your blessing remain with us throughout this day. Preserve us in Your righteousness, and grant us a portion in that eternal life which is in Christ Jesus, our Lord. Amen. (*LSB*, p. 309)

Morning

I thank You, heavenly Father, for Your protecting care and the refreshing sleep of this night. Graciously provide me with all the needs of the day, and guard me from sin, temptation, and every evil. Grant me wisdom and ability to serve You acceptably as I follow my chosen calling and perform my hourly tasks. Enable me to render some worthy service to my fellow men.

Washed from all my sin through the precious blood of my Savior, grant that the Holy Spirit direct my walk as becomes a Christian, and enable me to bear testimony of my faith by word and conduct.

Bless Your children in all places and under all conditions for the sake of Jesus. Amen.
(*TFT*, p. 212)

I thank You, my heavenly Father, through Jesus Christ, Your dear Son, that You have kept me this night from all harm and danger; and I pray that You would keep me this day also from sin and every evil, that all my doings and life may please You. For into Your hands I commend myself, my body and soul, and all things. Let Your holy angel be with me, that the evil foe may have no power over me. Amen.

As I stand at the threshold of this new day, I praise You, my Redeemer and Friend. Take me by the hand and lead me safely through my waking hours, protecting my soul from sin and Satan and giving me strength to perform my tasks acceptably to You and satisfactorily to my fellow men.

Give me grace to be forgiving and considerate, for You have forgiven me times without number.

Protect the children, keep the aged from stumbling and falling, ease the pains of the sick, put hope into the hearts of the distressed. Sustain us all and increase my faith, that I may grow in those Christian graces which do honor to You, my adorable Savior and constant Friend. Amen. (*TFT*, p. 214)

Eternal Caretaker of souls and Preserver of life, I arise to praise You with grateful heart for the protection I have enjoyed throughout the night. Today I again turn to You for guidance. In all that I do, let Your Word give me the directives.

As opportunity comes, give me the readiness to bear witness to Christ, my Savior, and let all that I say and do reveal Your love to those about me that belong to Your family.

Make me thoughtful, patient, and cheerful. Let me be helpful to others and make the journey more pleasant for all I meet on the highway of life. Enrich each hour of this day with Your presence and with Your benediction, for Jesus' sake. Amen. (*TFT*, p. 216)

Evening

Gracious Lord, we give You thanks for the
day, especially for the good we were permitted
to give and to receive. The day is now past,
and we commit it to You. We entrust to You
the night and rest in Your peace, for You are
our help and You neither slumber nor sleep.
Hear us for the sake of Your name. Amen.
(*LSB*, p. 309)

Evening

As the day comes to a close, O Lord God
Eternal, my heart and lips praise You with
songs of adoration as I bow to receive Your
benedictions. I am not worthy of this Your
grace, for I have not at all times done Your
will nor have I had the courage to bear
witness to the hope that is within me. In the
loving-kindness of Your heart, forgive me for
the sake of Jesus, who gave His life to wash
me of all uncleanness of my heart. Enrich
my life with Your heavenly peace that I may
enjoy a restful sleep, knowing that You are
watching over me. Let me awake tomorrow
with the resolve to serve You with greater
faithfulness by the power of the Holy Spirit.
Amen. (*TFT*, p. 211)

I thank You, my heavenly Father, through Jesus Christ, Your dear Son, that You have graciously kept me this day; and I pray that You would forgive me all my sins where I have done wrong, and graciously keep me this night. For into Your hands I commend myself, my body and soul, and all things. Let Your holy angel be with me, that the evil foe may have no power over me. Amen.

Evening

Lord God, eternal Caretaker of all, to You I also entrust my life and soul. In this changing world, You are always the same. The sun never sets upon Your love in Christ Jesus. With my failings and sins I come to Your Father heart seeking Your forgiveness in Jesus' cross. Fill my heart with peace and remove the worries that have bothered me this day.

Close out for the coming night all danger, and bless me with a refreshing sleep.

Lift the burdens from the weary, ease the pain of the suffering, protect those who are in danger on land and sea, give courage to the disheartened, and give the glory of Your Gospel to all who sit in spiritual darkness. In Jesus' name. Amen. (*TFT*, p. 213)

Evening

In this evening hour, heavenly Father, I am mindful of Your mercies and Your loving-kindness that has attended me each hour of this day. But, O Lord, I am fully conscious also of my many shortcomings and sins. I have not walked in Your perfect way. Forgive me for the sake of Jesus, who went to Calvary's cross to redeem me. Wash and heal me, and fill my troubled mind and heart with peace. Bless me with a refreshing sleep and graciously watch over me in my slumbers.

I commend all the children of men to You. Lead them to Calvary that they may share with me Your salvation in Christ Jesus. Then Yours shall be the glory and the praise in timeless eternity. Amen. (*TFT*, p. 217)

The "Mizpah" Prayer

Mizpah is a Hebrew word for "watchpost."

"The Lord watch between you and me, when we are out of one another's sight." Genesis 31:49

Almighty and eternal God, who promises Your divine presence to Your people wherever they be, graciously watch over us as we are away from one another. Protect us from dangers of the body and temptations of the soul.

Awaken in our hearts a deeper loyalty to one another and a greater faithfulness to You. Let our prayers unite at Your throne even though we be miles apart. Grant that as a family group we may again worship You and confess Jesus Christ as our Lord and Savior. Forgive us all our sins and preserve us in Your grace. Amen. (*TFT*, p. 219)

A Prayer for
Each Day of the Week

Sunday

Father, You made Sunday a day of rest. I know Sunday is a day of worship too. I don't always feel like worshiping You, Lord. Sometimes I'd rather sleep in or do something else that I enjoy more. When I do worship You, often my mind wanders. The devil surely is busy with distractions! I love You, Lord, despite my inattention during worship. Create in me a clean heart, O Lord—one that worships You. In Jesus' name. Amen.

Monday

Lord Jesus, it's off to school or off to work. I wish it were just off! Oh, I know You have blessed me with many things to do. Help me face this week with enthusiasm and encouragement. Give me a cheerful heart to face the many tasks required of me, and help me do well. In everything I do this week, help me do it to Your glory and according to Your will. For Jesus' sake. Amen.

Thank You, dear God, for giving me another
Tuesday. As I use the time You have given me,
help me think of others who don't know Your
love like I do. I need some ideas on how to
show these people Your love through what I
say and do. This Tuesday, I especially think of
_____ who always seems in need of help.
Help me be an answer to this prayer. Help
me to act on my belief in Your concern and
compassion for all people. Make me like Jesus,
in whose name I pray. Amen.

Wednesday

Happy Wednesday, Father! The middle of the
week is a good opportunity to worship You—
not just on Sunday. I praise You for all You've
done—creating the world and populating it
with people like me to take care of it—and for
using all Your power for my good. I especially
thank and praise You for sending Jesus to
take away my sins and for giving me the Holy
Spirit to help me grow in faith. I give thanks,
Lord, for You are indeed good. In fact, You are
the best. Keep me close to You forever. In my
Savior's name. Amen.

Thursday

It was a Thursday, dear Father, when Your Son, Jesus, met with His disciples to create what we now call the Lord's Supper. What a wonderful gift You gave them—and us—in Holy Communion. Each time I participate in the Lord's Supper, remind me of the forgiveness that Jesus earned for me. Remind me of the warm fellowship that Jesus had with those who believed in Him and the fellowship I have with other believers. For His holy name. Amen.

Friday

Thank You, God. It's Friday. Lots of people thank God it's Friday (TGIF, as some say), but I want to remember why I thank You. Yes, it's a good feeling to have the week behind me and the weekend ahead of me. But what makes Friday really great is that I remember what You did on Good Friday so long ago. Thank You for sending Jesus to suffer the punishment I deserve for my sins. Thank You for taking away my sins and leaving me with the sure promise of eternal life in heaven. Yes, thank You, God, for Friday. Let my life always celebrate this day—for the right reasons. For Your name's sake. Amen.

Lord God, how easy to forget prayer on Saturday! This day seems to belong to me alone. But I really don't want it that way. I want You to be with me. During the week, it's easy to know how much I need You. Yet I also need You on those days away from school, work, and other events that so easily stress me. I need You today. As I get away from the weekday routines, bring me close to You. Help me see how You're always with me, just as You promise in the Bible. In Jesus' name. Amen.

The Liturgy in Scripture

The Benedictus
(Zechariah's Song)

"Blessed be the Lord God of Israel,
   for He has visited and redeemed His people
and has raised up a horn of salvation for us
   in the house of His servant David,
as He spoke by the mouth of His holy
prophets from of old,

that we should be saved from our enemies and
from the hand of all who hate us;
to show the mercy promised to our fathers
   and to remember His holy covenant,
   the oath that He swore to our father
Abraham, to grant us
that we, being delivered from the hand of our
enemies,
might serve Him without fear,
   in holiness and righteousness before Him all
our days.
And you, child, will be called the prophet of
the Most High;
   for you will go before the Lord to prepare
His ways,
to give knowledge of salvation to His people
   in the forgiveness of their sins,
because of the tender mercy of our God,

whereby the sunrise shall visit us from on high
to give light to those who sit in darkness and in the shadow of death,
to guide our feet into the way of peace."

Luke 1:68–79

The Magnificat
(Mary's Song)

"My soul magnifies the Lord,
and my spirit rejoices in God my Savior,
for He has looked on the humble estate of His
servant.
   For behold, from now on all generations
will call me blessed;
for He who is mighty has done great things
for me,
   and holy is His name.
And His mercy is for those who fear Him
   from generation to generation.
He has shown strength with His arm;
   He has scattered the proud in the thoughts
of their hearts;
He has brought down the mighty from their
thrones
   and exalted those of humble estate;
He has filled the hungry with good things,
   and the rich He has sent empty away.
He has helped His servant Israel,
   in remembrance of His mercy,
as He spoke to our fathers,
   to Abraham and to his offspring forever."

Luke 1:46–55

The Nunc Dimittis
(Simeon's Song)

"Lord, now You are letting Your servant depart
in peace,
   according to Your Word;
for my eyes have seen Your salvation
that You have prepared in the presence of all
peoples,
a light for revelation to the Gentiles,
   and for glory to Your people Israel."

Luke 2:29–32

The Hymn of Praise
(This Is the Feast)

Then I looked, and I heard around the throne
and the living creatures and the elders the
voice of many angels, numbering myriads of
myriads and thousands of thousands, saying
with a loud voice, "Worthy is the Lamb who
was slain, to receive power and wealth and
wisdom and might and honor and glory
and blessing!" And I heard every creature in
heaven and on earth and under the earth and
in the sea, and all that is in them, saying,
"To Him who sits on the throne and to the
Lamb be blessing and honor and glory and
might forever and ever!" And the four living
creatures said, "Amen!" and the elders fell
down and worshiped.

Revelation 5:11–14

The Beatitudes

And He opened His mouth and taught them,
saying:
"Blessed are the poor in spirit, for theirs is the
kingdom of heaven.
"Blessed are those who mourn, for they shall
be comforted.
"Blessed are the meek, for they shall inherit
the earth.
"Blessed are those who hunger and thirst for
righteousness, for they shall be satisfied.
"Blessed are the merciful, for they shall receive
mercy.
"Blessed are the pure in heart, for they shall
see God.
"Blessed are the peacemakers, for they shall be
called sons of God.
"Blessed are those who are persecuted for
righteousness' sake, for theirs is the kingdom
of heaven.
"Blessed are you when others revile you
and persecute you and utter all kinds of evil
against you falsely on My account. Rejoice
and be glad, for your reward is great in
heaven, for so they persecuted the prophets
who were before you."   Matthew 5:2–12

Luther's Small Catechism

The Ten Commandments

As the head of the family should teach them in a simple way to his household

The First Commandment

You shall have no other gods.

What does this mean? We should fear, love, and trust in God above all things.

The Second Commandment

You shall not misuse the name of the Lord your God.

What does this mean? We should fear and love God so that we do not curse, swear, use satanic arts, lie, or deceive by His name, but call upon it in every trouble, pray, praise, and give thanks.

The Third Commandment

Remember the Sabbath day by keeping it holy.

What does this mean? We should fear and love God so that we do not despise preaching and His Word, but hold it sacred and gladly hear and learn it.

The Fourth Commandment

Honor your father and your mother.

What does this mean? We should fear and love God so that we do not despise or anger our parents and other authorities, but honor them, serve and obey them, love and cherish them.

The Fifth Commandment

You shall not murder.

What does this mean? We should fear and love God so that we do not hurt or harm our neighbor in his body, but help and support him in every physical need.

The Sixth Commandment

You shall not commit adultery.

What does this mean? We should fear and love God so that we lead a sexually pure and decent life in what we say and do, and husband and wife love and honor each other.

The Seventh Commandment

You shall not steal.

What does this mean? We should fear and love God so that we do not take our neighbor's money or possessions, or get them in any dishonest way, but help him to improve and protect his possessions and income.

The Eighth Commandment

You shall not give false testimony against your neighbor.

What does this mean? We should fear and love God so that we do not tell lies about our neighbor, betray him, slander him, or hurt his reputation, but defend him, speak well of him, and explain everything in the kindest way.

The Ninth Commandment

You shall not covet your neighbor's house.

What does this mean? We should fear and love God so that we do not scheme to get our neighbor's inheritance or house, or get it in a way which only appears right, but help and be of service to him in keeping it.

The Tenth Commandment

You shall not covet your neighbor's wife, or his manservant or maidservant, his ox or donkey, or anything that belongs to your neighbor.

What does this mean? We should fear and love God so that we do not entice or force away our neighbor's wife, workers, or animals, or turn them against him, but urge them to stay and do their duty.

[The text of the commandments is from Exodus 20:3, 7, 8, 12–17.]

The Close of the Commandments

What does God say about all these commandments? He says, "I, the Lord your God, am a jealous God, punishing the children for the sin of the fathers to the third and fourth generation of those who hate Me, but showing love to a thousand generations of those who love Me and keep My commandments." (Exodus 20:5–6)

What does this mean? God threatens to punish all who break these commandments. Therefore, we should fear His wrath and not do anything against them. But He promises grace and every blessing to all who keep these commandments. Therefore, we should also love and trust in Him and gladly do what He commands.

The Creed

As the head of the family should teach it in a simple way to his household

The First Article

Creation

I believe in God, the Father Almighty, Maker of heaven and earth.

What does this mean? I believe that God has made me and all creatures; that He has given me my body and soul, eyes, ears, and all my members, my reason and all my senses, and still takes care of them.

He also gives me clothing and shoes, food and drink, house and home, wife and children, land, animals, and all I have. He richly and daily provides me with all that I need to support this body and life.

He defends me against all danger and guards and protects me from all evil.

All this He does only out of fatherly, divine

goodness and mercy, without any merit or worthiness in me. For all this it is my duty to thank and praise, serve and obey Him.

This is most certainly true.

The Second Article

Redemption

And in Jesus Christ, His only Son, our Lord, who was conceived by the Holy Spirit, born of the Virgin Mary, suffered under Pontius Pilate, was crucified, died and was buried. He descended into hell. The third day He rose again from the dead. He ascended into heaven and sits at the right hand of God, the Father Almighty. From thence He will come to judge the living and the dead.

What does this mean? I believe that Jesus Christ, true God, begotten of the Father from eternity, and also true man, born of the Virgin Mary, is my Lord,

who has redeemed me, a lost and

condemned person, purchased and won me from all sins, from death, and from the power of the devil; not with gold or silver, but with His holy, precious blood and with His innocent suffering and death,

that I may be His own and live under Him in His kingdom and serve Him in everlasting righteousness, innocence, and blessedness,

just as He is risen from the dead, lives and reigns to all eternity.

This is most certainly true.

The Third Article

Sanctification

I believe in the Holy Spirit, the holy Christian church, the communion of saints, the forgiveness of sins, the resurrection of the body, and the life everlasting. Amen.

What does this mean? I believe that I cannot by my own reason or strength believe in Jesus Christ, my Lord, or come to

Him; but the Holy Spirit has called me by the Gospel, enlightened me with His gifts, sanctified and kept me in the true faith.

In the same way He calls, gathers, enlightens, and sanctifies the whole Christian church on earth, and keeps it with Jesus Christ in the one true faith.

In this Christian church He daily and richly forgives all my sins and the sins of all believers.

On the Last Day He will raise me and all the dead, and give eternal life to me and all believers in Christ.

This is most certainly true.

The Lord's Prayer

As the head of the family should teach it in a simple way to his household

Our Father, who art in heaven, hallowed be Thy name, Thy kingdom come, Thy will be done on earth as it is in heaven. Give us this day our daily bread; and forgive us our trespasses as we forgive those who trespass against us; and lead us not into temptation, but deliver us from evil. For Thine is the kingdom and the power and the glory forever and ever. Amen.

Our Father in heaven, hallowed be Your name, Your kingdom come, Your will be done on earth as in heaven. Give us today our daily bread. Forgive us our sins as we forgive those who sin against us. Lead us not into temptation, but deliver us from evil. For the kingdom, the power, and the glory are Yours now and forever. Amen.

The Introduction

Our Father who art in heaven.

Our Father in heaven.

What does this mean? With these words God tenderly invites us to believe that He is our true Father and that we are His true children, so that with all boldness and confidence we may ask Him as dear children ask their dear father.

The First Petition

Hallowed be Thy name.

Hallowed be Your name.

What does this mean? God's name is certainly holy in itself, but we pray in this petition that it may be kept holy among us also.

How is God's name kept holy? God's name is kept holy when the Word of God is taught in its truth and purity, and we, as the children of God, also lead holy lives according to it. Help us to do this, dear Father in heaven! But anyone who teaches or lives contrary to God's Word profanes the name of God among us. Protect us from this, heavenly Father!

The Second Petition

Thy kingdom come.

Your kingdom come.

What does this mean? The kingdom of God certainly comes by itself without our prayer, but we pray in this petition that it may come to us also.

How does God's kingdom come? God's kingdom comes when our heavenly Father gives us His Holy Spirit, so that by His grace we believe His holy Word and lead godly lives here in time and there in eternity.

The Third Petition

Thy will be done on earth as it is in heaven.

Your will be done on earth as in heaven.

What does this mean? The good and gracious will of God is done even without our prayer, but we pray in this petition that it may be done among us also.

How is God's will done? God's will is done when He breaks and hinders every evil plan and purpose of the devil, the world, and our sinful nature, which do not want us to hallow God's name or let His kingdom come; and when He strengthens and keeps us firm in His Word and faith until we die. This is His good and gracious will.

The Fourth Petition

Give us this day our daily bread.

Give us today our daily bread.

What does this mean? God certainly gives daily bread to everyone without our prayers, even to all evil people, but we pray in this petition that God would lead us to realize this and to receive our daily bread with thanksgiving.

What is meant by daily bread? Daily bread includes everything that has to do with the support and needs of the body, such as food, drink, clothing, shoes, house, home, land, animals, money, goods, a devout husband or wife, devout children, devout workers, devout and faithful rulers, good government, good weather, peace, health, self-control, good reputation, good friends, faithful neighbors, and the like.

The Fifth Petition

And forgive us our trespasses as we forgive those who trespass against us.

Forgive us our sins as we forgive those who sin against us.

What does this mean? We pray in this petition that our Father in heaven would not look at our sins, or deny our prayer because of them. We are neither worthy of the things for which we pray, nor have we deserved them, but we ask that He would give them all to us by grace, for we daily sin much and surely deserve nothing but punishment. So we too will sincerely forgive and gladly do good to those who sin against us.

The Sixth Petition

And lead us not into temptation.

Lead us not into temptation.

What does this mean? God tempts no one. We pray in this petition that God would guard and keep us so that the devil, the world, and our sinful nature may not deceive us or mislead us into false belief, despair, and other great shame and vice. Although we are attacked by these things, we pray that we may finally overcome them and win the victory.

The Seventh Petition

But deliver us from evil.

But deliver us from evil.

What does this mean? We pray in this petition, in summary, that our Father in heaven would rescue us from every evil of body and soul, possessions and reputation, and finally, when our last hour comes, give us a blessed end, and graciously take us from this valley of sorrow to Himself in heaven.

The Conclusion

For Thine is the kingdom and the power and the glory forever and ever. Amen.

For the kingdom, the power, and the glory are Yours now and forever. Amen.

What does this mean? This means that I should be certain that these petitions are pleasing to our Father in heaven, and are heard by Him; for He Himself has commanded us to pray in this way and has promised to hear us. Amen, amen means "yes, yes, it shall be so."

The Sacrament of Holy Baptism

As the head of the family should teach it in a simple way to his household

First

What is Baptism?

Baptism is not just plain water, but it is the water included in God's command and combined with God's word.

Which is that word of God?

Christ our Lord says in the last chapter of Matthew: "Therefore go and make disciples of all nations, baptizing them in the name of the Father and of the Son and of the Holy Spirit." (Matthew 28:19)

Second

What benefits does Baptism give?

It works forgiveness of sins, rescues from death and the devil, and gives eternal salvation to all who believe this, as the words and promises of God declare.

Which are these words and promises of God?

Christ our Lord says in the last chapter of Mark: "Whoever believes and is baptized will be saved, but whoever does not believe will be condemned." (Mark 16:16)

Third

How can water do such great things?

Certainly not just water, but the word of God in and with the water does these things, along with the faith which trusts this word of God in the water. For without God's word the water is plain water and no Baptism. But with the word of God it is a Baptism, that is, a life-giving water, rich in grace, and a washing of the new birth in the Holy Spirit, as St. Paul says in Titus, chapter three:

"He saved us through the washing of rebirth and renewal by the Holy Spirit, whom He poured out on us generously through Jesus

Christ our Savior, so that, having been justified by His grace, we might become heirs having the hope of eternal life. This is a trustworthy saying." (Titus 3:5–8)

Fourth

What does such baptizing with water indicate?

It indicates that the Old Adam in us should by daily contrition and repentance be drowned and die with all sins and evil desires, and that a new man should daily emerge and arise to live before God in righteousness and purity forever.

Where is this written?

St. Paul writes in Romans chapter six: "We were therefore buried with Him through baptism into death in order that, just as Christ was raised from the dead through the glory of the Father, we too may live a new life." (Romans 6:4)

Confession

How Christians should be taught to confess

What is Confession?

Confession has two parts.

First, that we confess our sins, and

second, that we receive absolution, that is, forgiveness, from the pastor as from God Himself, not doubting, but firmly believing that by it our sins are forgiven before God in heaven.

What sins should we confess?

Before God we should plead guilty of all sins, even those we are not aware of, as we do in the Lord's Prayer; but before the pastor we should confess only those sins which we know and feel in our hearts.

Which are these?

Consider your place in life according to the Ten Commandments: Are you a father, mother, son, daughter, husband, wife, or worker? Have you been disobedient, unfaithful, or lazy? Have you been hot-tempered, rude, or quarrelsome? Have you hurt someone by your words or deeds? Have you stolen, been negligent, wasted anything, or done any harm?

What is the Office of the Keys?

The Office of the Keys is that special authority which Christ has given to His church on earth to forgive the sins of repentant sinners, but to withhold forgiveness from the unrepentant as long as they do not repent.

Where is this written?

This is what St. John the Evangelist writes in chapter twenty: The Lord Jesus breathed on His disciples and said, "Receive the Holy Spirit. If you forgive anyone his sins, they are forgiven; if you do not forgive them, they are not forgiven." (John 20:22–23)

What do you believe according to these words?

I believe that when the called ministers of Christ deal with us by His divine command, in particular when they exclude openly unrepentant sinners from the Christian congregation and absolve those who repent of their sins and want to do better, this is just as valid and certain, even in heaven, as if Christ our dear Lord dealt with us Himself.

The Sacrament of the Altar

As the head of the family should teach it in a simple way to his household

What is the Sacrament of the Altar?

It is the true body and blood of our Lord Jesus Christ under the bread and wine, instituted by Christ Himself for us Christians to eat and to drink.

Where is this written?

The holy Evangelists Matthew, Mark, Luke, and St. Paul write:

Our Lord Jesus Christ, on the night when He was betrayed, took bread, and when He had given thanks, He broke it and gave it to the disciples and said: "Take, eat; this is My body, which is given for you. This do in remembrance of Me."

In the same way also He took the cup after supper, and when He had given thanks, He gave it to them, saying, "Drink of it, all of you; this cup is the new testament in My blood, which is shed for you for the forgiveness of sins. This do, as often as you drink it, in remembrance of Me."

What is the benefit of this eating and drinking?

These words, "Given and shed for you for the forgiveness of sins," show us that in the Sacrament forgiveness of sins, life, and salvation are given us through these words. For where there is forgiveness of sins, there is also life and salvation.

How can bodily eating and drinking do such great things?

Certainly not just eating and drinking do these things, but the words written here: "Given and shed for you for the forgiveness of sins." These words, along with the bodily eating and drinking, are the main thing in the a Sacrament. Whoever believes these words has exactly what they say: "forgiveness of sins."

Who receives this sacrament worthily?

Fasting and bodily preparation are certainly fine outward training. But that person is truly worthy and well prepared who has faith in these words: "Given and shed for you for the forgiveness of sins."

But anyone who does not believe these words or doubts them is unworthy and unprepared, for the words "for you" require all hearts to believe.

Daily Prayers

How the head of the family should teach his household to pray morning and evening

Morning Prayer

In the morning when you get up, make the sign of the holy cross and say:

In the name of the Father and of the ✠ Son and of the Holy Spirit. Amen.

Then, kneeling or standing, repeat the Creed and the Lord's Prayer. If you choose, you may also say this little prayer:

I thank You, my heavenly Father, through Jesus Christ, Your dear Son, that You have kept me this night from all harm and danger; and I pray that You would keep me this day also from sin and every evil, that all my doings and life may please You. For into Your hands I commend myself, my body and soul, and all things. Let Your holy angel be with me, that the evil foe may have no power over me. Amen.

Then go joyfully to your work, singing a hymn, like that of the Ten Commandments, or whatever your devotion may suggest.

Evening Prayer

In the evening when you go to bed, make the sign of the holy cross and say:

In the name of the Father and of the ✠ Son and of the Holy Spirit. Amen.

Then kneeling or standing, repeat the Creed and the Lord's Prayer. If you choose, you may also say this little prayer:

I thank You, my heavenly Father, through Jesus Christ, Your dear Son, that You have graciously kept me this day; and I pray that You would forgive me all my sins where I have done wrong, and graciously keep me this night. For into Your hands I commend myself, my body and soul, and all things. Let Your holy angel be with me, that the evil foe may have no power over me. Amen.

Then go to sleep at once and in good cheer.

How the head of the family should teach his household to ask a blessing and return thanks

Asking a Blessing

The children and members of the household shall go to the table reverently, fold their hands, and say:

The eyes of all look to You, [O Lord,] and You give them their food at the proper time. You open Your hand and satisfy the desires of every living thing. (Psalm 145:15–16)

Then shall be said the Lord's Prayer and the following:

Lord God, heavenly Father, bless us and these Your gifts which we receive from Your bountiful goodness, through Jesus Christ, our Lord. Amen.

Returning Thanks

Also, after eating, they shall, in like manner, reverently and with folded hands say:

Give thanks to the Lord, for He is good. His love endures forever. [He] gives food to every creature. He provides food for the cattle and for the young ravens when they call. His pleasure is not in the strength of the horse, nor His delight in the legs of a man; the Lord delights in those who fear Him, who put their hope in His unfailing love. (Psalm 136:1, 25; 147:9–11)

Then shall be said the Lord's Prayer and the following:

We thank You, Lord God, heavenly Father, for all Your benefits, through Jesus Christ, our Lord, who lives and reigns with You and the Holy Spirit forever and ever. Amen.

Table of Duties

Certain passages of Scripture for various holy orders and positions, admonishing them about their duties and responsibilities

To Bishops, Pastors, and Preachers

The overseer must be above reproach, the husband of but one wife, temperate, self-controlled, respectable, hospitable, able to teach, not given to drunkenness, not violent but gentle, not quarrelsome, not a lover of money. He must manage his own family well and see that his children obey him with proper respect. 1 Timothy 3:2–4

He must not be a recent convert, or he may become conceited and fall under the same judgment as the devil. 1 Timothy 3:6

He must hold firmly to the trustworthy message as it has been taught, so that he can encourage others by sound doctrine and refute those who oppose it. Titus 1:9

What the Hearers Owe Their Pastors

The Lord has commanded that those who preach the gospel should receive their living from the gospel. 1 Corinthians 9:14

Anyone who receives instruction in the word must share all good things with his instructor. Do not be deceived: God cannot be mocked. A man reaps what he sows. Galatians 6:6–7

The elders who direct the affairs of the church well are worthy of double honor, especially those whose work is preaching and teaching. For the Scripture says, "Do not muzzle the ox while it is treading out the grain," and "The worker deserves his wages." 1 Timothy 5:17–18

We ask you, brothers, to respect those who work hard among you, who are over you in the Lord and who admonish you. Hold them in the highest regard in love because of their work. Live in peace with each other. 1 Thessalonians 5:12–13

Obey your leaders and submit to their authority. They keep watch over you as men who must give an account. Obey them so that their work will be a joy, not a burden, for that would be of no advantage to you. Hebrews 13:17

Of Civil Government

Everyone must submit himself to the governing authorities, for there is no authority except that which God has established. The authorities that exist have been established by God. Consequently, he who rebels against the authority is rebelling against what God has instituted, and those who do so will bring judgment on themselves. For rulers hold no terror for those who do right, but for those who do wrong. Do you want to be free from fear of the one in authority? Then do what is right and he will commend you. For he is God's servant to do you good. But if you do wrong, be afraid, for he does not bear the sword for nothing. He is God's servant, an agent of wrath to bring punishment on the wrongdoer. Romans 13:1–4

Of Citizens

Give to Caesar what is Caesar's, and to God what is God's. Matthew 22:21

It is necessary to submit to the authorities, not only because of possible punishment but also because of conscience. This is also why you pay taxes, for the authorities are God's servants, who give their full time to governing. Give everyone what you owe him: If you owe taxes, pay taxes; if revenue, then revenue; if respect, then respect; if honor, then honor. Romans 13:5-7

I urge, then, first of all, that requests, prayers, intercession and thanksgiving be made for everyone—for kings and all those in authority, that we may live peaceful and quiet lives in all godliness and holiness. This is good, and pleases God our Savior. 1 Timothy 2:1-3

Remind the people to be subject to rulers and authorities, to be obedient, to be ready to do whatever is good. Titus 3:1

Submit yourselves for the Lord's sake to every authority instituted among men: whether to the king, as the supreme authority, or to governors, who are sent by him to punish those who do wrong and to commend those who do right 1 Peter 2:13–14

To Husbands

Husbands, in the same way be considerate as you live with your wives, and treat them with respect as the weaker partner and as heirs with you of the gracious gift of life, so that nothing will hinder your prayers. 1 Peter 3:7

Husbands, love your wives and do not be harsh with them. Colossians 3:19

To Wives

Wives, submit to your husbands as to the Lord. Ephesians 5:22

They were submissive to their own husbands, like Sarah, who obeyed Abraham and called him her master. You are her daughters if you do what is right and do not give way to fear. 1 Peter 3:5–6

To Parents

Fathers, do not exasperate your children; instead, bring them up in the training and instruction of the Lord. Ephesians 6:4

To Children

Children, obey your parents in the Lord, for this is right. "Honor your father and mother"— which is the first commandment with a promise—"that it may go well with you and that you may enjoy long life on the earth." Ephesians 6:1–3

To Workers of All Kinds

Slaves, obey your earthly masters with respect and fear, and with sincerity of heart, just as you would obey Christ. Obey them not only to win their favor when their eye is on you, but like slaves of Christ, doing the will of God from your heart. Serve wholeheartedly, as if you were serving the Lord, not men, because you know that the Lord will reward everyone for whatever good he does, whether he is slave or free. Ephesians 6:5–8

To Employers and Supervisors

Masters, treat your slaves in the same way.
Do not threaten them, since you know that
He who is both their Master and yours is in
heaven, and there is no favoritism with Him.
Ephesians 6:9

To Youth

Young men, in the same way be submissive
to those who are older. All of you, clothe
yourselves with humility toward one another,
because, "God opposes the proud but gives
grace to the humble." Humble yourselves,
therefore, under God's mighty hand, that He
may lift you up in due time. 1 Peter 5:5–6

To Widows

The widow who is really in need and left all
alone puts her hope in God and continues
night and day to pray and to ask God for help.
But the widow who lives for pleasure is dead
even while she lives. 1 Timothy 5:5–6

To Everyone

The commandments . . . are summed up in
this one rule: "Love your neighbor as your-
self." Romans 13:9

I urge . . . that requests, prayers, intercession
and thanksgiving be made for everyone.
1 Timothy 2:1

*Let each his lesson learn with care, and all the
household well shall fare.*

Prayers for each day of the week are from *Teens Pray: Conversations with God* by Edward Grube, copyright © 2002 Concordia Publishing House. All rights reserved.

Cover Photo: Shutterstock

This publication may be available in braille, in large print, or on cassette tape for the visually impaired. Please allow 8 to 12 weeks for delivery. Write to Lutheran Blind Mission, 7550 Watson Rd., St. Louis, MO 63119-4409; call toll-free 1-888-215-2455; or visit the Web site: www.blindmission.org.

Library of Congress Cataloging-in-Publication Data

Blessings and prayers for Confirmation : a devotional companion.

    p. cm.

 ISBN 978-0-7586-1608-1

1. Confirmation--Prayers and devotions. I. Title.

BV815.B54 2009

242'.8041--dc22

2008025674

2 3 4 5 6 7 8 9 10 11   22 21 20 19 18 17 16 15 14 13